D1524829

FAST CARS

LOTUS

by Jameson Anderson

Reading Consultant:
Barbara J. Fox
Reading Specialist
North Carolina State University

Content Consultant:
Gary David
Cleveland Area Lotus, Ltd.
Cleveland, Ohio

Capstone
press

Mankato, Minnesota

Blazers is published by Capstone Press,
151 Good Counsel Drive, P.O. Box 669, Mankato, Minnesota 56002.
www.capstonepress.com

Library of Congress Cataloging-in-Publication Data
Anderson, Jameson.
  Lotus / by Jameson Anderson.
  p. cm. — (Blazers. Fast cars)
  Summary: "Simple text and colorful photographs describe the history and
models of the Lotus" — Provided by publisher.
  Includes bibliographical references and index.
  ISBN-13: 978-1-4296-1280-7 (hardcover)
  ISBN-10: 1-4296-1280-0 (hardcover)
  1. Lotus automobile — Juvenile literature. I. Title. II. Series.
TL215.L67A53 2008
629.222'2 — dc22   2007033123

Editorial Credits
Angie Kaelberer, editor; Bobbi J. Wyss, designer; Jo Miller, photo researcher

Photo Credits
Alamy/Motoring Picture Library, 12; Phil Talbot, 13, 14 (bottom), 28–29;
    Popperfoto, 8; Transtock Inc., 5
AP Images/Andy Wong, 27
Corbis/Schlegelmilch, 22
The Image Works/National Motor Museum/HIP, 18
iStockphoto/Jan Paul Schrage, 15 (bottom), 17
Ron Kimball Stock/Ron Kimball, cover, 6, 21
SuperStock, Inc., 11, 14 (top)
ZUMA Press/Stan Sholik, 15 (top), 25

Essential content terms are **bold** and are defined at the bottom of the page
where they first appear.

1 2 3 4 5 6 13 12 11 10 09 08

TABLE OF CONTENTS

chapter 1

MEET THE LOTUS

It's the day of a huge car show. A shiny sports car rolls into the parking lot. The sleek look of the Lotus wows everyone who sees it.

1999 Lotus Elise

2002 Lotus Esprit

Many sports cars are known more for speed than for comfort. But Lotus cars are so comfortable that some models are known as *luxury* cars.

> *luxury* — something that is not needed but adds great ease and comfort

Colin Chapman

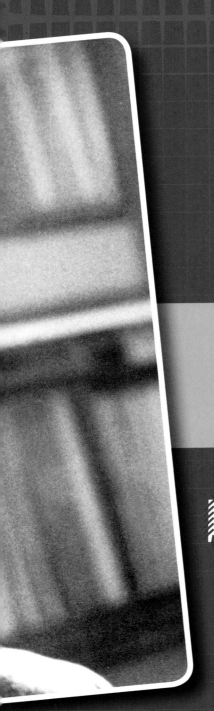

chapter 2

LOTUS HISTORY

Colin Chapman built the first Lotus *model* in 1948. It was called the Mark I.

model — a specific type of car

Chapman introduced the Lotus Seven in 1957. This two-seat sports car quickly became one of the most popular Lotus models.

fast fact

The Seven was also sold as a kit for buyers to build themselves.

Lotus Seven

Lotus Elan coupe

In 1962, Lotus introduced the Elan roadster. It was the first Lotus road car to have a ***backbone chassis***. This chassis was narrower than other frames.

backbone chassis — a very narrow hollow steel structure that supports the engine and other parts

In 1966, Lotus produced the Europa. It was the first mass-produced sports car with a mid-sized engine. The Europa was designed to drive like a Formula One race car.

Lotus Europa

LOTUS TIMELINE

The Lotus Seven is introduced.

1957

Colin Chapman dies at age 54.

1982

1948

1966

Colin Chapman builds the Mark I.

Lotus releases the Europa.

Lotus body styles have changed a lot since Chapman built the Mark I. Today's smooth designs help the cars go faster.

The Exige is released.

2000

1996

2007

Lotus shows off the Exige GT3 concept car.

The Elise is introduced.

chapter 3

FAST AND LIGHT

Lotus cars are lightweight. The Lotus Elise weighs just 1,984 pounds (900 kilograms). Most sports cars weigh twice as much.

fast fact

The Elise was named after a past company chairman's granddaughter.

Lotus Elise Series 2

1962 Lotus Elite

To make the Lotus weigh as little as possible, most of the body is made of **fiberglass**. The 1962 Lotus Elite even had a fiberglass chassis.

fiberglass — a strong, lightweight material made of thin threads of glass

Lotus engine size changes with the model. The Lotus Elise has a small four-*cylinder* engine. Yet it roars down the road at 150 miles (240 km) per hour.

cylinder — a hollow area inside an engine in which fuel burns to create power

2006 Lotus Exige engine

Lotus 49 Formula One race car in
the 1969 British Grand Prix

chapter 4

A RACING MACHINE

For many years, Lotus had its own Formula One race team. The Lotus team won the World Championship six times.

fast fact

Famous U.S. Formula One driver Mario Andretti raced for Team Lotus in the late 1970s.

In 2000, Lotus introduced the Exige. The 2007 Exige S model zips from zero to 60 miles (97 km) per hour in about four seconds.

2007 Lotus Exige S

chapter 5

FULL SPEED AHEAD

Today, Lotus engineers are working with an electric car company named ZAP. Together, they are building a super-fast electric car. Will it be Lotus' next big hit?

PRO

fast fact

The ZAP car will use the Aluminum Performance Crossover (APX) body. Lotus presented this stylish concept car in 2006.

The ZAP car will look like the APX car (above).

LOTUS DIAGRAM

air scoop

spoiler

T836 AVC
KINGS

roll bar

air duct

fiberglass body

alloy wheel

29

GLOSSARY

backbone chassis (bak-BOHN CHA-see) — a very narrow hollow steel structure that supports the engine and other parts

concept car (KON-sept KAR) — a vehicle built to show off an idea

cylinder (SIL-uhn-dur) — a hollow area inside an engine in which fuel burns to create power

engineer (en-juh-NIHR) — someone who designs and builds machines, vehicles, or other structures

fiberglass (FYE-bur-glass) — a strong, lightweight material made from thin threads of glass

luxury (LUHG-zhuh-ree) — something that is not needed but adds great ease and comfort

mass-produce (mas-pruh-DOOS) — to make cars in a large quantity using machinery

model (MOD-uhl) — a specific type of car

sleek (SLEEK) — smooth and shiny

READ MORE

Maurer, Tracy Nelson. *Lotus*. Full Throttle. Vero Beach, Fla.: Rourke, 2007.

Schuette, Sarah L. *Formula One Cars*. Horsepower. Mankato, Minn.: Capstone Press, 2007.

Sutton, Richard. *Car*. DK Eyewitness Books. New York: DK Publishing, 2005.

INTERNET SITES

FactHound offers a safe, fun way to find Internet sites related to this book. All of the sites on FactHound have been researched by our staff.

Here's how:
1. Visit *www.facthound.com*
2. Choose your grade level.
3. Type in this special code **1429612800** for age-appropriate sites. You may also browse subjects by clicking on letters, or by clicking on pictures or words.
4. Click on the **Fetch It** button.

FactHound will fetch the best sites for you!

INDEX